One You Love
Has Died

*Ideas for How Your Grief
Can Help You Heal*

To Paul,
friend always

I am indebted to Carrie Hackney, Beth Beams, John Peterson, Jennifer Levine, Clare Barton, Sue Devito, and, as always, my wife Bernie Miller, for their constructive thoughts following the initial writing of this book. The perspective each of them has brought to this work has made it more accurate, more readable, and more usable.

Willowgreen Publishing
10351 Dawson's Creek Blvd., Suite B
Fort Wayne, Indiana 46825
260/490-2222

www.willowgreen.com

ISBN 1-885933-29-0

Someone you've been close to has died. It may be a family member or friend, someone you've worked with or someone in your care. However long you've known this person, you've grown attached to them. And now they are gone, and it hurts.

If you're like many people in our culture, you're unsure about what's expected of you now. You're new to the role of "griever" and you haven't been very well prepared for your part. There was a time, just a few generations ago, when a book like this would have been laughable. No one would have read it because everyone knew what to expect of grief and how to act as a griever. Grief's rituals were many and obvious, clearly a part of everyday life. Grief's importance was understood.

Today, however, it's a different story. There are few universally accepted practices that help people through the process of grief. Except for what happens in the first few days following a death, bereaved people are not given much guidance or permission to do their mourning. In fact, sometimes there's very little assistance even in those first hours and days. Consequently, many people today don't know what to expect. They're unsure what they should do. They're given conflicting advice by others. They're in the dark as to what the future holds. Perhaps that's the case with you.

This book is designed to help you understand and become more comfortable with your grief. It's meant to support and encourage you during a difficult and perhaps unsteady time of your life. It's also meant to show you the possibilities of what can happen, especially the possibility of how you can heal. I hope that will be true for you—that your time of grief will be a time of healing and of hope.

Jim Miller

To love is to be vulnerable.
Love anything and your heart will certainly be wrung
and possibly broken.

C. S. LEWIS

❧

Where you used to be, there is a hole in the world,
which I find myself constantly walking around
in the daytime, and falling into at night.

EDNA ST. VINCENT MILLAY

❧

The eager fate which carried thee
Took the largest part of me:
For this losing is true dying.

RALPH WALDO EMERSON

1

You're likely to have various feelings as you grieve, and it helps when you can do something with them.

"Sorrow makes us all children again," said the revered poet Ralph Waldo Emerson. He would know. His wife died after two years of marriage. Later his six-year-old son died three days after contracting scarlet fever. He wrote in his journal after his son's death that he doubted if he could ever love anything or anyone again.

When someone you love dies, you too may feel that your grief makes you like a child again. Your feelings may be closer to the surface. Your emotions may overpower you when you least expect them to, or for reasons you don't fully understand. You may feel as if you're on an emotional roller coaster and you don't know when or where this ride will come to an end.

Your feelings may be many.

It's common, of course, for people to feel sad after the death of someone close. Endings are sorrowful experiences. In fact, this may be the saddest time you've ever known. It's possible you feel depressed or in despair. You may be facing doubts like Emerson about ever being able to love again, or be happy again.

You may find you're more anxious than normal, or more afraid, and about things that never affected you before. You may feel extremely lonely. Even worse, your loneliness may increase when you're around others, even those who care about you. You may feel embarrassed or ashamed of how you're acting as you grieve, or for how long you're grieving, even if it seems natural for you to grieve in the ways you do.

Most people in your situation report that they're constantly tired, which makes complete sense—grief is *very* hard work. You may feel helpless, as if you've lost control of your life, or at least certain parts of it. You may get angry more easily than normal. You may focus your anger on what has happened to you, on those around you, on yourself, or on God. You may even get mad at the person who died, for what they did to you, for instance, or for how they deserted you, however logical or illogical those feelings may be.

Another common response is guilt—guilt for what you did or didn't do when your loved one was alive, or at the time of their death, or perhaps after they died. Some people experience a sense of relief when their loved one dies, which can be quite understandable in certain circumstances, and then they may feel guilty for feeling relieved.

You may experience gratitude or satisfaction or joy as you look back upon this person's life and the time you spent together. You may feel hopeful as you anticipate what can lie ahead, both for them and for you.

Another possibility is that you may not feel much at all. You may be numb for awhile, even a long while. You may feel removed from your emotions. A few weeks after his son's death, Emerson wrote, "I chiefly grieve that I cannot grieve." Sometimes that happens.

What you *do* with your emotions will vary.

Whatever you do with your emotions, never underestimate the value of simply feeling what you feel, and feeling it as fully as you can. In doing that, you give your emotions the importance and the attention they deserve. Just staying with your feelings for awhile, or mulling them over by yourself, can mean you're doing a great deal.

Putting your feelings into words almost always helps. Research shows that having at least one other person with whom you can talk about your grief is one of the healthiest steps you can take. Do you have a family member, a friend, or a co-worker with whom you can share your thoughts and feelings? Can you do this regularly, and especially during particularly trying times? Perhaps there are several people to whom you can turn. Sometimes a professional—a chaplain, counselor, minister, or physician—can be a good sounding board. Grief support groups are another option.

Your words may come out in ways other than by talking. Some people enjoy writing. If you're like that, you might want to keep a journal so you can capture what's going on inside, as well as monitor your progress over time. You can write letters to someone you know and describe what's happening. If you choose, you can write the one who died—such letters can be valuable releases, even though you're not able to send them. You may express yourself in verse. You can reminisce on paper, telling stories that are worth preserving for yourself or some future generation.

Some of your feelings may not come out in words at all—they may lie beyond words. Crying can be a very effective expression of sorrow. You may wish to draw or paint what's inside you. You may carve or photograph, weave or sew, work with clay or wood. If you're so inclined, you might sing your grief or your hope. You might play a musical instrument. Sometimes just listening to certain kinds of music can help free and confirm your feelings. So can reading certain kinds of books or articles, or watching particular videos or movies. Praying your feelings can be a liberating experience too. Some people have found meaning in turning the reading of the Psalms into their own personal prayer.

This may all seem very strange to you.

You may feel as if you're no longer who you once were. A woman whose son died in a tragic accident put it this way: she felt as if she had lost her old self and she wondered if that former self, one she rather liked, would ever return. Many people who are grieving also speak about feeling different from those around them and not "fitting in" the way they once did. Perhaps those are your feelings too. If they are, know you're not alone.

But also know that your feelings, all of them, are a natural part of your grieving process. They're a sign of how human you are, how much you're involved in life, how much you love the person who died, and how much you miss that person. Your feelings are terribly important. So treat them that way. Give them your time, your attention, your respect.

Grief is a matter of relativity;
the sorrow should be estimated
by its proportion to the sorrower;
a gash is as painful to one
as an amputation is to another.

PERCY BYSSHE SHELLEY

When you are sorrowful look again in your heart,
and you shall see that in truth you are weeping
for that which has been your delight.

KAHLIL GIBRAN

How do you expect to arrive
at the end of your journey
if you take the road to another one's city?

THOMAS MERTON

2

You'll grieve in your own unique way, and a general pattern will emerge as you do so.

Those around you may be full of ideas about how you're supposed to grieve, and how not. You may be told that grief comes in clear-cut stages and you may even be given a name for the stage you're supposedly in. You may hear advice like *"Be strong!"* or *"Cheer up!"* or *"Get on with your life!"* rather than be encouraged to allow your grief to run its natural course. It's important for you to be clear that this is *your* grief, not theirs. You'll grieve in no one's way but your own.

Grief can affect your mind and body.

Grief is about more than your feelings—it will also show up in how you think. You may disbelieve this person actually died. You may have episodes of thinking like this even long after they died. Your mind may be confused, your thinking muddled. You may find it difficult to concentrate on just about everything. Or you may be able to focus your attention but all you can focus on is the one who died, or how they died, or your life together before they died.

Physical responses are also to be expected. You may experience tightness in your throat, heaviness across your chest, or pain around your heart. Your stomach may be upset, along with other intestinal disturbances. You may have headaches, hot flashes, or cold chills. You may be dizzy at times, or tremble more than usual, or find yourself easily startled. Some people find it hard to get their breath.

You may undergo changes in your behavior. You may sleep less than you used to and wake up at odd hours. Or you may sleep *more* than normal. You may have odd dreams or frightening nightmares. You may become unusually restless. You may move from one activity to another, sometimes not finishing one thing before moving on to the next. Or you may sit and do nothing for long periods. Some people engage in what's called "searching behavior"—you look for your loved one's face among a crowd of people, for instance, even though you know they've died. You may become attached to things you associate with your loved one, like wearing an article of their clothing or carrying a keepsake that belonged to them. Or you may wish to avoid all such reminders.

Grief can affect your relationships and everyday activities.

Many grieving people want to spend more time alone. Sometimes they're drawn to the quiet and safety they experience there, and sometimes it's a way of dodging other people. Even venturing out to the grocery store, a shopping mall, or a worship service can feel uncomfortable. There are some people, however, who want to be around others even more than before.

You may find that you're jealous of people around you who aren't grieving. You may envy what they have that you don't. You may resent how much they take for granted when you now realize that *nothing* should ever be taken for granted. You may become critical in ways that are unlike you. Fortunately, this shift is usually temporary.

Some grieving people report unusual happenings that are not easy to describe yet seem very real. You may be going about your daily life and suddenly have a sense of your loved one's presence. Some people report having auditory or visual experiences related to this person. Sometimes the loved one offers a message during a dream or time of meditation. Try not to worry if something like this should happen to you once in a while. Such experiences are more common than you might think. Usually these times are comforting.

Research also indicates that people's responses during times of personal loss will be influenced by how they're raised, their genetic make-up, and society's expectations. Consequently, some people are naturally more feeling-oriented as they grieve, while others are more oriented toward using their thinking processes. Some respond outwardly, while others keep to themselves. Some want to have a close network of friends around them, and others prefer to be independent. Ordinary, healthy grief has many possible faces and can express itself in many different ways. You are your own person, with your own personality, your own life experiences, your own relationship with the one who died, and your own understanding of life and death. So you should not expect a "one-size-fits-all grief" that will suit you. You're too unique for that.

Generally a pattern will unfold.

Despite your individual uniqueness, you'll probably discover an overall pattern to your grief as it progresses. It often begins with a time of shock and numbness, especially if the death was sudden. Everything seems unreal. This is usually followed by a time when pain sets in. Sadness, loneliness, helplessness, and fear may come over you in powerful waves. Anger and guilt may do the same, and continue for awhile. In time there comes a slowly growing acceptance of what has happened, but it's not necessarily a happy acceptance. It's common to feel listless and lifeless, discouraged and sometimes depressed. Other strong emotions can still pop up. This is the winter of your grief—a long, slow, dormant period. In actuality, something is beginning to grow, but it's hidden deep underground.

A time of gradual reawakening eventually occurs, though you can't always predict when. Energy begins to return. So does hope. Finally there comes a time of renewed life. You're not the same person you were before—you'll be different, having been changed by this experience, having grown. You'll forge a new relationship with the one who died, a relationship that transcends time.

This entire process is very fluid. It may not feel very orderly. These time periods will flow into one another almost imperceptibly. But when you look back, you'll recognize what's happened: by going all the way through your grief, you've taken the path toward your healing.

Our remedies oft in ourselves do lie,
Which we ascribe to heaven.

WILLIAM SHAKESPEARE

⋅◦◦⋅

You alone can do it,
but you cannot do it alone.

O. HOBART MOWRER

⋅◦◦⋅

Those whom we support
hold us up in life.

ANNE SOPHIE SWETCHINE

⋅◦◦⋅

It is sweet to mingle tears with tears;
Griefs, when they wound in solitude,
Wound more deeply.

SENECA

3

It's important to take good care of yourself, while allowing others to care for you.

Grief depletes you. It robs you of your strength, your energy, your confidence. It can diminish your sense of self-esteem. It isolates you from others, and maybe from yourself. It can become one of the most stress-filled times of your life, if not *the* most stress-filled. And stress, of course, can affect you in many ways, including heightened blood pressure and lowered immunity to disease, to name just two. That's why it's important to see to it that you receive good care during this time.

However much you'd like that care to come from others, the truth is that some care can come only from yourself. Some things are impossible for others to do, no matter how sensitive or loving those people are. They cannot cry your tears or confront your fears for you. They cannot shield you from anniversaries or holidays. They cannot take away your pain. Sometimes those around you don't know what you need, or they may hesitate to step forward due to the awkwardness they feel. For those and other reasons, you may wish to place your care in the hands of someone who's especially knowledgeable about what you need—you.

You can oversee your own care.

It helps to pay attention to the basics as you move through your time of mourning. Eat balanced meals. If your taste for food has disappeared, eat anyway, knowing how important your nutrition is at a time like this. Drink plenty of water. Be wise and responsible about the use of alcohol and other agents that affect your body and influence your behavior. Monitor your weight. If you haven't had a physical examination recently, get one.

Exercise regularly, at least three or four times a week. Walk, swim, jog, or cycle. Do aerobics. Lift weights. Go rollerblading. Try whatever works for you and feels right for you. It's been proven that exercise helps you feel better mentally as well as physically.

Get the rest you need. Develop habits that encourage your nightly sleep. Nap if you want. Give yourself time to sit and relax or to read and ponder. Go easy on your self-imposed expectations and responsibilities.

Do things that bring you pleasure, even if that pleasure is muted for the moment. Make time for people you enjoy, those with whom you feel comfortable. Spend time in nature—if not every day, then at least several times a week. Try doing projects with your hands—it can help quiet your mind while providing you with a sense of accomplishment. Give yourself little presents from time to time, like something new to wear, a favorite treat to taste, a bouquet of flowers to enjoy, or anything else that cheers you. If you want and if you enjoy it, do small things for other people. It often helps to concentrate on needs beyond your own.

In as many ways as seem appropriate, determine what would be beneficial and healing for you and then act to make it happen. Of course, that may mean giving yourself permission to kick back and do nothing at all for awhile. That can be healing too.

Others may want to show they care.

Allowing other people to do things with you and for you during this time is not at all a sign of weakness or deficiency on your part. Allowing yourself to lean a little is a sound way of getting through this difficult time with as much health and human understanding as possible. So let other people show they care. Allow them to serve as a stabilizing influence in a time which may seem rather unstable. Accept that you are worth the attention and nurturing that other people may want to give you. Permit a sense of community to form around you if it wants to.

Keep in mind that those who volunteer to help may need to do that for themselves as much as for you. If they're grieving the same death you are, this can be an important way for them to deal with that loss themselves. If what saddens them is simply *your* sadness, then one way they can handle their concern is to find ways to assist you and to show that their hearts are beside yours. Inevitably, those around you will feel a certain helplessness, as you may well understand.

Accept as many of their offers as feels right. Be gracious with any refusals on your part and let people know you'll entertain other offers in the future. If someone says, "Let me know if there's anything I can do," then take them at their word and let them know. Be specific about what would help. Ask people to do those things they feel most competent doing. And while you'll want to express your appreciation, don't feel you must overdo it. Remember you're in this experience together. You're both helping and you're both being helped at the same time.

Take this sorrow to thy heart,
and make it a part of thee,
and it shall nourish thee
till thou art strong again.

HENRY WADSWORTH LONGFELLOW

⚬⚬⚬

Winter is come and gone,
But grief returns with the revolving year.

PERCY BYSSHE SHELLEY

⚬⚬⚬

We are healed of a suffering
only by experiencing it to the full.

MARCEL PROUST

4

You're likely to encounter other losses as you grieve, and that can be useful.

When someone you love dies, you expect to grieve the ending of their life as well as the relationship the two of you have built together. You expect to miss doing what you've enjoyed doing with each other and sharing whatever you liked to share. But whether you anticipate it or not, you may become aware that other losses keep cropping up as you deal with this present loss.

A primary loss creates a wave of secondary losses.

You already know what a primary loss is, and you've learned it the hard way. That's a loss that hurts a great deal, one that really shakes up your life, one you're likely to remember as long as you live. Such losses seldom appear by themselves—they bring with them other losses which may not seem as serious as the first, but they can still be serious enough. And the cumulative effect of these other losses can be substantial.

Take, for example, the case of a man whose wife died after thirty years of happy marriage. Her death is likely to feel devastating to him and he will grieve that lost relationship deeply. But as he begins to adapt, he will miss more than just his partner in marriage. He may feel as if he's lost his best friend. If they had children, he'll be without her support and influence as a parent. If she worked outside the home, he'll lose a source of income. He may need to move to a different home. Some of their friends may drop away, especially if their social life had been couple-oriented or if his wife had been the one to organize such times. He'll lose his sexual partner, as well as the person who performed so many chores around their home, some of which he may have no idea how to perform himself. That's a lot of losses.

Another example is a woman whose only child has died. In addition to that awful loss, there will be other ones—her role and identity as mother, many of her daily routines, a significant source of her love, and perhaps her sense of security, her faith, or her dreams for the future. She may lose some closeness with her husband for awhile, or some feeling of normalcy with her friends.

Every momentous loss brings in its wake a series of other losses. Sometimes those are immediately recognized and sometimes it takes a while before you see them. Whenever those other losses appear, they become a part of that central experience of your grief. It's critically important that you pay attention to these so-called secondary ones. Why? Because each of them needs and deserves its own separate grief response. By grieving about all that's happened—the little things as well as the larger ones—then your whole grief experience becomes more understandable, more manageable. This can help you adjust to what has happened to you the best way possible—bit by bit, a little at a time.

Another's death may bring past losses to the fore.

When author Anne Morrow Lindbergh's older sister Elizabeth died at barely thirty years of age, Anne found she was taken back to the heavy grief associated with the killing of her son two years before. Eight years later with the death of Thor, the German shepherd that had protected the Lindbergh family after the baby's death, once again the previous losses surfaced for her. That's a common phenomenon. One death brings back the memory and feelings associated with previous deaths. Such life-changing events are too important to be neglected or forgotten.

Yet it's more than death-related experiences that can return—so can those experiences related to all kinds of losses. For the truth is that any loss represents a kind of dying, even if it's only a little death, a partial death, or a temporary death. Anyone who's been through a painful separation or divorce may be taken back to some of that pain as he or she mourns the death of another. You may find yourself focusing on an abortion that took place or a child given in adoption if that has been a part of your story. You may remember when you lost your possessions in a calamity, or your health through a serious illness, or some part of your body in an accident.

These past losses need not resemble the present one. It's not the external similarities that matter so much as the internal ones—the familiar fears, disappointments, and sorrows, as well as the unknown future.

Any death may bring up unresolved losses.

There may be losses in your life with which you're not yet at peace. Maybe there hasn't been enough time to adjust to the previous death or misfortune when this most recent one occurred. Or maybe there has been plenty of time but for one reason or another the healing has still not taken place. If you've not fully grieved an earlier loss in your life, this present death may serve as an invitation for it to present itself again so it can be attended to and worked through. Sometimes these uncompleted losses go back many, many years. A situation in which this commonly occurs is with the death of a parent or sibling when a child is quite young. Unable to appreciate the true nature of death and therefore the full experience of grief, that child will need to grieve more times as she or he reaches new levels of maturity.

Secondary, previous, and unresolved losses will give you extra things to deal with as you grieve. But they will also give you more opportunity to grow into a mature human being and to assimilate what has happened to you on a deeper level. Perhaps you'll find value in seeking out someone who's trained to help you sort through the complexities of this time. Whatever you choose to do, remember there's a quiet wisdom at work in your grief. Something deep within wants to help you be more whole.

God will not look you over
for medals, degrees or diplomas,
but for scars.

ELBERT HUBBARD

❦

Amid my list of blessings infinite,
Stands this the foremost,
"That my heart has bled."

EDWARD YOUNG

❦

A Death blow is a Life blow to Some
Who till they died, did not alive become—
Who had they lived, had died but when
They died, Vitality begun.

EMILY DICKINSON

5
A time of grief is a time of challenges, which can help you stretch and grow.

Despite the popularity of the saying "Time heals all wounds," it's not exactly true. Time by itself will not heal the gash that has been created by the death of the one you love. Your healing is not simply a matter of waiting things out, of letting enough time pass by until you feel good again. True healing happens only after you get involved yourself.

This active involvement is not easy. It hurts to grieve. The way before you is not always clear. The ground around you may not feel firm. You may have doubts about what you're to do and how you're to do it, or even *if* you can do it. Grief is a very challenging process. It demands your determination, perseverance, and ingenuity. Although your grief experience—and therefore your challenges—will be uniquely yours, following are some of the more common challenges.

You may wonder why people aren't more understanding.

People may not give you much opportunity to say what's on your mind and in your heart. They may say things that don't feel good and don't help you, like "I know exactly how you feel" when they really don't because they really can't—they're not you. They may think they're encouraging you by saying, "Oh, it could be worse," when really they're discounting the seriousness of what has happened to you. They may avoid the subject of your grief altogether, acting as if nothing really happened. They may even avoid *you* altogether.

There can be many reasons why people act this way. They may not know any better because something like this has never happened to them. They may feel awkward and not know what else to say or do except offer a standard cliché. They may be focused on themselves, fearing what would happen to them in a similar situation. Then again, they may just be acting thoughtlessly.

Try to keep in mind that we're all products of our culture and that most segments of modern North American culture don't deal very well with death and grief—we're deficient in that way. Be forgiving when you can, but also be firm when you feel you must, letting people know when they're hurting rather than helping your process. Assert your personal right to grieve.

You may wonder if you can do what is yours to do.

Once I telephoned a friend across country when I learned her son had been killed in an auto accident the night before. Her first words to me were, "Jim, I'm not sure I can do this." You may resonate with her sentiment. You may not be sure you can bear the pain, or muster the strength, or go through the days ahead. Your grief may require a new kind of courage for you—a courage unseen by others, when you face time and again what has happened, when you allow yourself to feel fully what this loss means for you. This can only be done slowly, gradually, and achingly, perhaps only one day at a time or even one hour at a time. It can only be done when you find your own personal ways to connect with that pain rather than always push it away from you. There's wisdom in Robert Frost's words, "The best way out is always through." With patience, understanding, and love—and your full share of courage—you can meet the challenge of going entirely through your grief. That's one way you find the power to move on *beyond* your grief.

You may wonder if you're going a little crazy.

Looking back on the period following her husband's death, actress Helen Hayes said, "I was just as crazy as you can be and still be at large." Many grieving people wonder at one time or another if they're going a little nutty, or maybe a *lot* nutty. You may act in unusual ways and think unusual thoughts. Keep this in mind: a time of wrenching loss creates a very unusual time in your life. To act completely usual in a situation that's terribly *unusual* is, well, unusual. To put it another way: if from time to time you feel a little crazy as you move through the chaos of your grief, that can be a decent sign you're fairly sane.

You may wonder if your faith will survive this.

Some people find their convictions shaken as a result of a grave loss. Perhaps you're one of them. You may question life's fairness or God's justice or maybe even God's existence. "Why did this have to happen?" you may ask. "Why the one I love? Why me? Why now?"

If such questions form within you, don't feel you must hide them or put them off. Be aware there's a long and honorable tradition of voicing one's doubts as well as expressing one's outrage toward the Divine. Your honest questioning can be a step toward achieving a more mature faith and a more enriching spirituality.

You may wonder if your mourning will ever end.

Grief has a way of hanging on longer than you expect. You may wonder if you'll ever feel good again. When your grief presents you with so many unknowns, you may find it difficult to trust the direction it's leading you. But that's usually what will help you most—trusting the process of your grief.

When you go ahead and do what your grief asks of you, you will almost always be led to another place in your life, a brighter place than you now find yourself. When you roll up your sleeves and get involved in the workings of your grief, you will begin to be changed by what you're doing. In time you'll move toward feeling life's fullness again, although that doesn't mean you'll return to being exactly the way you once were. You will feel normal again, but it will be a *new* normal— a normal that's forged out of what you've been through and all you've done.

Your challenges will test you and stretch you as you move through your grief. But in this very testing and stretching, a gift will be left with you. You'll begin to feel more capable, more empowered, more sure. You'll begin to sense you're healing.

Learn weeping, and thou shalt gain laughing.

GEORGE HERBERT

❧

*What we have once enjoyed and deeply loved
we can never lose,
for all that we love deeply
becomes a part of us.*

HELEN KELLER

❧

*The human heart does not obey the rules of logic:
it is constitutionally contradictory.
I can truly say that I have a great grief
and that I am a happy man.*

PAUL TOURNIER

6
Your time of grief has its possibilities.

While there is much you may not enjoy about your time of grief, it does not have to be only an awful experience. And while this period of your life will have its full share of sadness, that need not be its only characteristic. This experience of living on after another has died may hurt, but something more than hurting can happen too.

Your grief can be a time of heightened awareness.

You may find what others have found—that being in grief is like living in another world. That world is sparser, quieter, somewhat removed. After you've been in this world for awhile, your perceptions begin to change. You become aware of things you might not notice if you were living through a busier and happier period of your life. Many people who are grieving report that, among other things, they become more appreciative of life's little blessings.

You may feel especially grateful for small acts of kindness—a telephone call at just the right moment, a note in the mail with just the right message, an invitation to dinner with just the right people. You may feel suddenly connected with the universe upon hearing the sweet song of a bird or upon seeing the rays of a morning sun. Perhaps a cherished memory will quietly lift you or a meandering walk through God's creation may quietly ground you. You may come to realize these little moments of serendipity aren't so little after all, and it is your grief that can help teach you that lesson.

Your grief can be a time of discovery.

Serious loss has a way of pushing your limits and expanding your horizons. When that happens, any number of discoveries can await you. You may learn, for instance, how much you mean to others, and how much others mean to you. You may experience the power of forgiveness or the surprising freedom of honesty. You may find out where your strengths lie or where

25

your values rest. You may come to see what gives your life meaning as you've never seen it, because now you're face-to-face with it. You may uncover some of grief's paradoxes—how it's possible to gain in the very act of losing, for example, or how there's a "hello" to be said with every "good-bye."

Your grief can be a time of re-ordered priorities.

When someone who has been very close to you dies, especially if their death has been unexpected or untimely, you may be led to reflect upon how you've lived life so far, and how you want to live it from here on out. This can become a time of personal examination: *In light of what has happened, what is really important to me now? What do I want to invest my time and energy in, while I still have both? What worries am I ready to release? What joys do I want to grasp? What dreams will I now follow?* This can become a crossroads experience for you.

Your grief can be a time of re-formed connection.

When another dies, your task is not so much to sever the bonds you shared as to find ways to reconstitute those bonds. It entails not so much relinquishing your relationship with the one you loved as building a different kind of relationship with the one you *still* love. It's not possible for that person to be beside you any longer, but they can still be with you—they can be *inside* you. The ancient Persian poet Rumi described it this way as he grieved the death of his dearest friend: "Now that you live here in my chest, anywhere we sit is a mountaintop." Rumi's experience can be yours.

Your grief can be a time of hope.

Grief itself is a marvel. With little prompting, it helps you move from a former period of your life to a future period. It begins with death, and it refuses to hide from death. Yet as grief progresses, it leads you in the direction of death's opposite—it leads you toward life. That's its purpose, its goal. And that means that grief itself is a source of hope. That means that anyone who has grieved successfully can be a source of hope too.

What can you hope for as you grieve? You can hope you'll grow from this experience, more than just be changed by it. You can hope you'll be able to put what has happened to positive use someday, maybe for yourself, maybe for others, maybe even for the one who died. Perhaps the most significant hope you can harbor is this: that if your hope has left you, it will one day return. In addition, you can hope that someone will hold your hope for you until you can carry it again yourself.

Your grief can be a time of love.

At its best, this can be a time when you learn what real love is about. It transcends time and space—all time and all space, both on earth and beyond earth. Your grief can be a time when love flows in all directions—to the one who has died, to those who grieve with you, to others who care for you, to yourself. At its best, your love turns into a sense of compassion for anyone and everyone. When that happens, love is not something you do but someone you're becoming.

Seen in these ways, grief is about much more than death and loss. It's also about life and hope. It's about memories and bonds. It's about possibilities.

The question is not: why did this happen,
or where is it going to lead you,
or what is the price you will have to pay.
It is simply: how are you making use of it.

DAG HAMMARSKJOLD

⟐

Only people who are capable of loving strongly
can also suffer great sorrow,
but this same necessity of loving
serves to counteract their grief
and heals them.

LEO TOLSTOY

The Conclusion, and the Way Forward

Whatever has occurred in your life, you have some command over what happens from this point forward. You may not feel that way at the moment. Your life and your grief may seem far beyond your control. If your loved one's death has been quite recent or especially tragic, it may be awhile before you can believe that you're not entirely at the mercy of what's happened. But ultimately you *do* have choices, and if not today, then tomorrow.

You can choose if you will allow yourself to go through the pain of your grief, or if instead you will avoid that pain at all costs. In allowing yourself to tap into that pain in the manner and with the rhythm that seem right for you, then you can gradually make your way through your grief so that eventually you'll be on the far side of it.

You can choose whether or not you will put yourself in a position so that your grief can do its work as healthfully and as naturally as possible. Will you provide good self-care? Will you allow others to care? Will you allow yourself to learn as you go? Will you open yourself to what others have learned before you? Will you trust the process?

There is another choice you have and it's been best described by Viktor Frankl, an Austrian psychotherapist and World War II concentration camp survivor. Every member of Frankl's family died in the gas chambers, including his beloved pregnant wife. He came close to dying himself. One thing that kept him alive, he said, and that permitted him to rise above these events, was the freedom that he claimed as he went through these experiences—"the freedom to choose one's attitude in any given set of circumstances."

Like Frankl, you can choose the attitude you bring to this experience of loss. Will you see it only as a catastrophe, or can it somehow be a challenge, something that may call you forward? Will this death be a dead end in your life, or can it hold some sort of possibility, even if you have little idea at the moment what that possibility might be? Will you see your life now as broken, or might it become broken open in some life-giving way? Will you see this event as only robbing you, or might it some day leave you something of value?

This freedom to choose is yours and it cannot be taken from you. So may you, like Frankl, freely choose the attitude you take toward your loss.

May you see in this death a beckoning toward life, however subtle that beckoning may be.

May you see in this losing the possibility of a gaining, however much you wish you didn't have to gain in this way.

May you see in your grieving the potential it holds—the potential for your deepened loving, your gradual healing, and your continued awakening.

May you be able to say with the anonymous Chilean poet,

> *I have loved.*
> *I have been loved.*
> *The sun has carressed my face.*
> *Life, you owe nothing.*
> *Life, we are at peace.*

Books by James E. Miller

Welcoming Change
Discovering Hope in Life's Transitions

Autumn Wisdom
Finding Meaning in Life's Later Years

The Caregiver's Book
Caring for Another, Caring for Yourself

When You Know You're Dying
12 Thoughts to Guide You Through the Days Ahead

One You Love Is Dying
12 Thoughts to Guide You on the Journey

When You're Ill or Incapacitated / When You're the Caregiver

What Will Help Me? / How Can I Help?

How Will I Get Through the Holidays?
12 Ideas for Those Whose Loved One Has Died

Winter Grief, Summer Grace
Returning to Life After a Loved One Dies

A Pilgrimage Through Grief
Healing the Soul's Hurt After Loss

Helping the Bereaved Celebrate the Holidays
A Sourcebook for Planning Educational and Remembrance Events

Effective Support Groups
How to Plan, Design, Facilitate, and Enjoy Them

The Art of Being a Healing Presence
A Guide for Those in Caring Relationships

The Rewarding Practice of Journal Writing
A Guide for Starting and Keeping Your Personal Journal

When A Man Faces Grief / A Man You Know Is Grieving

Videotapes by James E. Miller

Invincible Summer
Returning to Life After Someone You Love Has Died

Listen to Your Sadness
Finding Hope Again After Despair Invades Your Life

How Do I Go On?
Re-designing Your Future After Crisis Has Changed Your Life

Nothing Is Permanent Except Change
Learning to Manage Transition in Your Life

By the Waters of Babylon
A Spiritual Pilgrimage for Those Who Feel Dislocated

We Will Remember
A Meditation for Those Who Live On

Gaining a Heart of Wisdom
Finding Meaning in the Autumn of Your Life

Awaken to Hope
Affirming Thoughts to Begin Your Day

Be at Peace
Assuring Thoughts to End Your Day

The Natural Way of Prayer
Being Free to Express What You Feel Deep Within

You Shall Not Be Overcome
Promises and Prayers for Uncertain Times

The Grit and Grace of Being a Caregiver
Maintaining Your Balance While You Care for Others

Why Yellow?
A Quiet Search for That Which Lies Behind All That Is

Common Bushes Afire
Discovering the Sacred in Our Everyday Lives

For additional information contact
Willowgreen Publishing
10351 Dawson's Creek Blvd., Suite B
Fort Wayne, Indiana 46825
260/490-2222
jmiller@willowgreen.com